cooking with wine

Fiona Beckett

cooking with wine

Photography by **William Lingwood**

RYLAND
PETERS
& SMALL

LONDON NEW YORK

Designers Saskia Janssen and
Anna Murphy
Editor Sharon Cochrane
Production Sheila Smith
Art Director Gabriella Le Grazie
Publishing Director Alison Starling

Food Stylist Annie Rigg
Prop Stylist Helen Trent

First published in the United States
in 2005
by Ryland Peters & Small, Inc.
519 Broadway, 5th Floor
New York, NY 10012
www.rylandpeters.com

10 9 8 7 6 5 4 3 2 1

Library of Congress Cataloging-in-
Publication Data

Beckett, Fiona.
  Cooking with wine / Fiona Beckett ;
photography by William Lingwood.
       p. cm.
  Includes index.
  ISBN 1-84172-954-X
  1. Cookery (Wine) I. Title.
  TX726.B367 2005
  641.6'22--dc22
                              2005008174

Notes

• All spoon measurements are level
  unless otherwise stated.

• Eggs are large unless otherwise
  specified. Uncooked or partly
  cooked eggs should not be
  served to the very old, frail,
  young children, pregnant women,
  or those with compromised
  immune systems.

contents

a splash of wine

As a wine lover, I always seem to have a couple of opened bottles in the kitchen. Wine is as natural an addition to my cooking as olive oil. I add a quick splash to the pan to make an instant sauce for steak, pour a glass into the tin when I cook a roast, use the best part of a bottle to cook a slow, flavorsome braise, or sweeten it to make a fabulous fruit jelly. There are so many different ways to use it.

Wine adds flavor, first of all. It makes an everyday dish special, whether it's a simple tomato sauce or a stew. It adds a beautifully balanced acidity to a cream sauce or, when reduced to a few intense spoonfuls, a marvellous sauce of its own. There are so many different flavors present in wine that can accent a dish—the sharpness of a lemony Sauvignon, the bright red berries of a Merlot or Cabernet, the luscious orange zestiness of a Muscat can all be used to reinterpret classic dishes such as poached salmon, coq au vin, or syllabub.

However, there is one myth that I need to destroy which is that you can use any old leftover wine in your cooking. It's not true. If you add a wine that's been open for too long, your recipe won't benefit from it at all. You don't have to use the best wine for your cooking (though you can always borrow a glass from a bottle you're planning to drink), but it must be clean and fresh and, it goes without saying, not corked. Young, fruity wines generally work better than mature, oak-aged ones and don't use that bottle you've had tucked away for years.

So do join me and get into cooking with wine. It's one of the easiest and most enjoyable ways to give your food that extra edge and really impress your friends.

appetizers

1¹/₄ cups crisp, dry white wine, such as Pinot Grigio

2 garlic cloves, very finely chopped

2 bay leaves

1 tablespoon coriander seeds

1 teaspoon coarse sea salt, plus extra for seasoning

¹/₂ teaspoon black peppercorns

¹/₄–¹/₂ teaspoon crushed dried chiles, to taste

¹/₃ cup extra virgin olive oil

1–2 tablespoons freshly squeezed lemon juice

2 small zucchini

12 oz. button mushrooms

2 heaping tablespoons chopped fresh mint leaves

2 heaping tablespoons chopped fresh parsley

freshly ground black pepper

warm pita bread or other flatbread, to serve

Serves 4

This dish offers a modern twist to the classic French way of serving a vegetable salad with a hot wine-based dressing. I like to pour the dressing over the vegetables rather than cook them in it, which makes for brighter colors and a fresher, crunchier texture. Tone down the heat by using fewer chiles, if you prefer.

zucchini & mushrooms
à la Grècque

Heat the wine, garlic, and bay leaves in a small saucepan and simmer gently until the wine has reduced by half. Remove and discard the bay leaves. Grind the coriander seeds, sea salt, peppercorns, and dried chiles using a pestle and mortar. Add this to the reduced wine, along with the olive oil and 1 tablespoon lemon juice. Stir and simmer over very low heat for 4 to 5 minutes.

Meanwhile, top and tail the zucchini and cut them lengthwise into very thin slices using a mandolin or a vegetable peeler. Wipe the mushrooms and slice them thickly. Put the zucchini and mushrooms in a large, heatproof serving bowl, pour over the hot dressing, and sprinkle with the mint leaves. Toss the vegetables in the dressing, then let cool for about 1 hour, tossing them occasionally.

Check the seasoning, adding more salt, pepper, and lemon juice, if necessary. Add the parsley, toss well, and serve with warm pita bread or other flatbread.

Recommended wine match Try a simple, crisp, fresh white—the same wine used to make the dish would be fine. A dry rosé would also work really well.

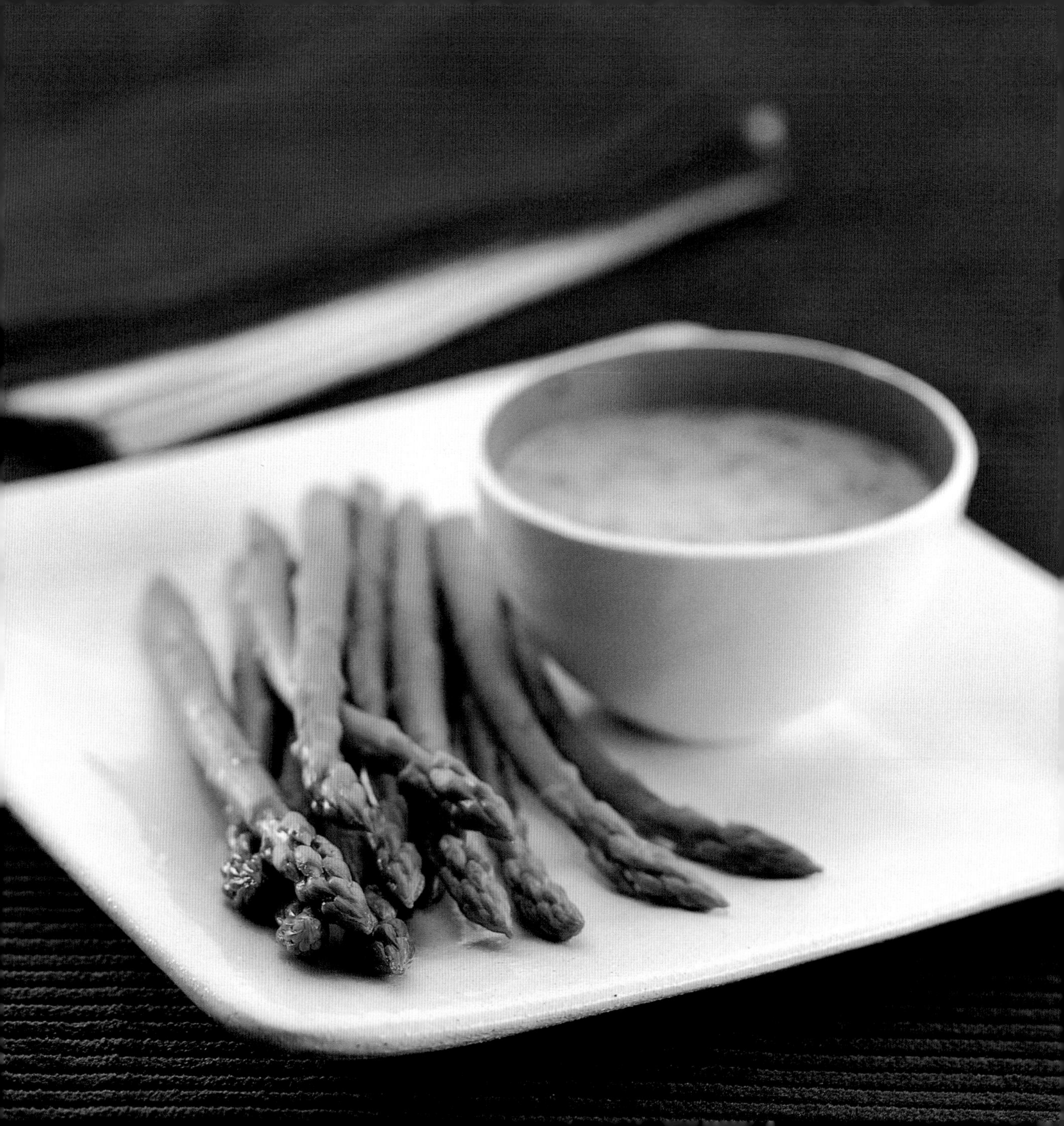

This really easy yet impressive-looking sauce is a version of the French beurre
blanc, *which consists of adding butter to a white wine reduction. Since the taste
of the butter is crucial, buy the best unsalted butter you can find. Go for a citrus-
flavored Sauvignon Blanc from somewhere like California, Chile, or Australia's
Adelaide Hills region rather than one with a gooseberry flavor.*

steamed asparagus
with **sauvignon**, lemon, & dill sauce

Rinse the asparagus and trim the stalks. Put them in the basket of an asparagus steamer or
a regular steamer and steam for about 5 minutes until the stems are just tender. Remove
the steamer from the heat and take off the lid.

Meanwhile, put the wine and finely chopped shallot in a non-reactive (stainless steel)
saucepan and cook over medium to low heat until the liquid has reduced by half. Reduce
the heat as low as possible and beat in the chilled butter a few cubes at a time with a wire
whisk. As the butter is incorporated and the sauce thickens, beat in a few more cubes until
it has all been added. Season to taste with a small squeeze of lemon juice and salt and
pepper, then stir in the dill.

To serve, put the asparagus spears on warm plates and spoon the warm sauce over the
tips or serve it separately.

Recommended wine match You could either stick to Sauvignon Blanc or drink an
unwooded or lightly oaked Chardonnay.

**2 small bunches of asparagus,
about 1 lb. in total**

**3 tablespoons Sauvignon Blanc
or other citrus-flavored
white wine**

**1 shallot, very finely chopped
(as finely as possible)**

**1 stick very good quality
unsalted butter, chilled and
cut into small cubes**

**1 teaspoon freshly squeezed
lemon juice**

**1 tablespoon finely chopped
fresh dill**

**sea salt and freshly ground
white pepper**

Serves 4

It may seem wantonly extravagant to use champagne in your cooking, but you only need a glass and the bonus is that you can drink the rest with the risotto. I suggest using a Blanc de Noirs, if you can get hold of one—it has just the right toasty richness for this recipe. The combination of champagne, mushrooms, and Parmesan is sublime.

wild mushroom & champagne risotto

8 oz. wild mushrooms or
8 oz. cremini mushrooms and
1 oz. dried porcini, soaked for
15 minutes in warm water

2 tablespoons light olive oil

6 tablespoons unsalted butter

5¹/₂ cups light chicken or
vegetable broth

1 medium onion,
finely chopped

1¹/₃ cups risotto rice, such as
arborio or carnaroli

¹/₂ cup champagne or other
sparkling white wine

3 heaped tablespoons freshly
grated Parmesan cheese

sea salt and freshly ground
black pepper

Serves 6

Clean the fresh mushrooms by lightly brushing or wiping them with a damp cloth, then slice them thinly. Drain the porcini, if using, and slice them. Reserve the soaking water.

Heat a medium skillet, add half the oil and half the butter, and fry the sliced fresh mushrooms briefly until lightly browned, about 4 minutes. Remove the pan from the heat, cover, and set aside.

Heat the broth in a saucepan until almost boiling, then reduce the heat and let simmer.

Meanwhile, heat the remaining oil and half the remaining butter in a large, heavy-based saucepan. Add the onion and cook over low heat for 4 to 5 minutes until soft. Increase the heat slightly, add the rice to the pan, and stir until well coated with the butter and the grains turn opaque, about 3 minutes.

Add the champagne or other sparkling wine to the pan—it will sizzle and evaporate almost immediately. Add the sliced porcini, if using, then begin adding the hot broth, a large ladle at a time, stirring gently until the liquid has been almost absorbed by the rice. Add the next ladle of broth and repeat until the rice is tender and creamy but still has some "bite" to it. This should take 15 to 20 minutes.

About 5 minutes before the end of the cooking time, stir in most of the fresh mushrooms, reserving a few for serving. When the risotto is ready, stir in the remaining butter and the Parmesan and season to taste with salt and pepper. If you've used dried porcini, add 1 to 2 tablespoons of the strained soaking water for extra flavor. Cover the pan and let the risotto relax for a few minutes while you reheat the reserved mushrooms. Serve the risotto in warmed bowls with a few sautéed mushrooms sprinkled on top.

Cooking scallops is a bit like cooking a steak. You can sear them over high heat, then make a delicious hot dressing with a dash of wine mingled with the pan juices. You can make this with just the pancetta for an easy, everyday meal, but the parsnip chips turn it into a glamorous dinner party starter.

warm scallop salad
with crispy pancetta & parsnip chips

To make the parsnip chips, peel the parsnip and cut off the root end to leave a piece about 4 inches long and 1½ inches wide at its narrowest point. Using a mandolin or a vegetable peeler, shave off very thin slices from the parsnip. Fill a wok about one-quarter full with vegetable oil and heat until very hot, about 375°F, or until a cube of bread turns golden in 40 seconds. Fry the parsnip slices, in batches, until brown and crisp, 30 to 60 seconds. Remove the chips with a slotted spoon, drain them on paper towels, and sprinkle lightly with salt.

Season the scallops on both sides with salt and pepper. Heat 1 tablespoon olive oil in a skillet, add the cubed pancetta, and sauté, turning occasionally, until crisp, 3 to 4 minutes. Remove the pancetta from the pan with a slotted spoon, drain on paper towels, then set it aside and keep warm.

Pour off the fat from the skillet, then return it to the heat for about 1 minute until almost smoking. Add the scallops to the pan and cook for 2 to 3 minutes, depending on their thickness, turning them over halfway through. Remove them from the pan, set aside, and keep them warm.

Pour the white wine into the pan and let it bubble up. Continue cooking until the wine has reduced by half. Add the fish broth or water and keep the liquid bubbling until it has reduced to just over a couple of tablespoons. Pour any juices that have accumulated under the scallops into the pan, stir in the cream or crème fraîche, and season to taste with salt and pepper. Warm through for a few seconds, then remove the pan from the heat.

Divide the salad greens between 4 plates, drizzle with a little olive oil, and season lightly with salt and pepper. Scatter over the pancetta and the parsnip chips. Put 3 scallops on each plate, spoon the pan juices over them, and serve immediately.

12 large fresh scallops, shelled

1 tablespoon olive oil, plus extra for dressing the salad

3½ oz. pancetta, cubed

¼ cup Chardonnay, Viognier, or other full-bodied white wine

2 tablespoons fish broth or water

1 tablespoon heavy cream or crème fraîche

mixed salad greens, about 3 oz.

sea salt and freshly ground black pepper

Parsnip chips

1 medium parsnip, about 7 oz.

vegetable oil, for deep-frying

Serves 4

This classic bistro dish is a wonderful way to enjoy mussels. The French would generally use a basic white vin de table, *but I think it tastes particularly good with Muscadet.*

moules à la marinière
with muscadet

2¼ lb. fresh mussels

3 tablespoons light olive oil or canola oil

1 medium onion, finely chopped

2 garlic cloves, finely chopped

½ cup Muscadet or other crisp dry white wine

3 heaped tablespoons chopped fresh parsley

To serve, your choice of:

French fries and mayonnaise

crusty bread

Serves 2

Tip the mussels into a sink full of cold water and give them a good swirl. Drain off the water, fill up the sink again, and swirl the mussels once more. Discard any mussels that are open. Using a small, sharp knife, remove the hairy "beards." Transfer the cleaned mussels to a large bowl of fresh, cold water.

Heat the oil in a large saucepan or deep casserole, add the chopped onion, and cook over low heat for 5 to 6 minutes until beginning to soften. Stir in the garlic, pour in the wine, then increase the heat and bring to a boil. Drain the mussels and tip them into the pan. Turn them over in the sauce, cover the pan, and cook over high heat for 3 minutes, shaking the pan occasionally. Remove the lid and check the mussels are open. If not, cover and cook for 1 minute more. Discard any mussels that haven't opened, then sprinkle over the parsley.

Serve immediately in deep bowls accompanied by fries and mayonnaise (wickedly delicious), or crusty bread.

Recommended wine match The remaining Muscadet would go well, or use any simple, carafe-style French white.

Red wine can be used in place of wine vinegar to make a deliciously fruity salad dressing. I've suggested Pinot Noir here, but you could use any other medium-bodied, fruity red wine. Making a red wine reduction like this is a thrifty way to use up leftover wine, and it will keep in the refrigerator for several days. If you can't find a fresh pomegranate, you could use sun-dried cherries instead.

smoked duck, tangerine, & pecan salad
with **pinot noir** & pomegranate dressing

Peel and slice the tangerines horizontally, reserving any juice. Cut the larger slices in half to make half-moon shapes.

To make the dressing, put the wine in a small saucepan, bring it to a boil, then lower the heat. Simmer for 10 to 15 minutes or until the wine has reduced by two-thirds (leaving about 6 tablespoons). Remove the pan from the heat, stir in the sugar, and let cool.

Once cool, whisk in the olive oil and season to taste with salt and pepper. Cut the pomegranate in half and scoop the seeds into a bowl, catching any juice. Discard the pith and tip the seeds and juice, along with any juice from the tangerines, into the dressing. Add the pomegranate molasses or balsamic vinegar, to taste. Stir well.

Divide the lamb's lettuce or watercress between 6 plates and arrange the duck breast and tangerine slices on top. Scatter over the candied pecans or walnuts. Give the dressing a quick whisk, then spoon it over the salad. Serve immediately.

***Note** If you can't find candied pecans, put ²/₃ cup pecans in a dry, nonstick skillet and sprinkle over 1 teaspoon sugar. Toast gently over medium heat for a couple of minutes, shaking the pan frequently, until the nuts are crisp and the sugar has caramelized.

Recommended wine match The dressing is quite intense, so choose an equally powerful New World Pinot Noir from, for example, Chile, California, Oregon, or Central Otago in New Zealand to stand up to it.

3 tangerines or small sweet oranges

4 oz. lamb's lettuce (mâche) or watercress

8 oz. sliced smoked duck breast

²/₃ cup candied pecans* or walnuts

Pinot Noir & pomegranate dressing

1 cup Chilean or other inexpensive Pinot Noir, or another fruity red wine

1¹/₂ tablespoons light brown sugar

¹/₂ cup light olive oil

1 medium pomegranate

¹/₂–1 teaspoon pomegranate molasses or balsamic vinegar

sea salt and freshly ground black pepper

Serves 6

fish & seafood

The combination of white wine, tomatoes, and basil is an Italian classic, so it seems in the spirit of the recipe to use an Italian wine like Pinot Grigio, but any crisp, dry white will do. Serve with some boiled rice or crisp sautéed zucchini for a deliciously light, quick supper dish for two.

quick tiger shrimp
with **pinot grigio**, fresh tomato, & basil sauce

3 tablespoons olive oil

8 oz. raw tiger shrimp, thawed if frozen

1 small onion or 2 shallots, very finely chopped

1 garlic clove, crushed

about 1/2 cup Pinot Grigio or other crisp, dry white wine

12 oz. vine-ripened tomatoes, peeled*, then roughly chopped

a small pinch of sugar

8 fresh basil leaves, torn

sea salt and freshly ground black pepper

boiled rice, to serve

Serves 2

Heat 2 tablespoons oil in a skillet or wok, add the shrimp, and sauté briefly until they turn pink. Remove them from the pan with a slotted spoon and set aside.

Add the remaining oil to the pan, then add the onion or shallots and sauté for 1 to 2 minutes until softened but not browned. Stir in the garlic, then pour in the wine and cook until it has almost evaporated. Add the tomatoes and their juice and cook for 4 to 5 minutes, breaking them up with a fork or spatula to make a thick sauce. Add the sugar, season to taste with salt and pepper, then stir in the basil leaves. Return the shrimp and any accumulated juices to the pan and heat through gently. Serve immediately with boiled rice.

***Note** To peel tomatoes, cut a cross in the bottom of each one using a small, sharp knife. Put the tomatoes in a heatproof bowl and cover them with boiling water. Let stand for about 1 minute, then remove them with a slotted spoon. When cool enough to handle, peel off the skins.

Recommended wine match Try a glass of the same wine that is used to make the dish—preferably a crisp, dry Italian white, such as Pinot Grigio.

Cooking with wine has the image of being calorific, but this fresh tasting, zingy fish dish couldn't be lighter. This is a modern adaptation of the French technique of poaching fish called a court-bouillon, *which leaves the salmon deliciously moist and fragrantly spiced.*

thai spiced salmon
with cucumber & cilantro salad

Fit the salmon fillets snugly in a single layer in the bottom of a large saucepan. Pour over the white wine and enough cold water to cover the fish, then remove the salmon fillets and set aside. Add the garlic, ginger, lemongrass, cilantro stalks, kaffir lime leaves, and peppercorns to the pan and bring to a boil. Add the salt, reduce the heat, and simmer for 15 minutes.

Gently slide the salmon fillets into the pan ensuring they are completely covered with the broth, if not, add more boiling water to cover. Bring the broth back to a boil and cook for 2 minutes. Remove the pan from the heat, cover, and let cool completely—at least 5 hours or overnight.

To make the cucumber and cilantro salad, put the lime juice, fish sauce, garlic, ginger, and chile in a bowl and mix well. Add 2 to 3 tablespoons water and season to taste with pepper and sugar (it shouldn't need any salt). Add the cucumber, bell pepper, carrot, scallions, cilantro, and mint leaves and toss well. Serve the salmon fillets accompanied by the salad and a few lime wedges for squeezing over.

Recommended wine match I often enjoy this zingy fresh dish without wine, but a bone dry Riesling from Germany, Austria, or Alsace works very well with these flavors.

4 thick salmon fillets, 5 oz. each

1¼ cups dry white wine, such as Pinot Grigio or Muscadet

2 garlic cloves

a small chunk of ginger, peeled and thickly sliced

1 stalk of lemongrass, cut into 3

a few fresh cilantro stalks

6 fresh or dried kaffir lime leaves

8 peppercorns

½ teaspoon sea salt

1 lime, cut into wedges, to serve

Cucumber & cilantro salad

freshly squeezed juice of 2 limes

1½ tablespoons fish sauce

1 garlic clove, crushed

1-inch piece of ginger, peeled and grated

1 small red chile, seeded and very finely chopped

½–1 teaspoon sugar

⅓ cucumber, peeled, seeded, and thinly sliced

1 green bell pepper, seeded and very thinly sliced

1 large carrot, quartered and cut into very thin strips

3 scallions, thinly sliced

3 tablespoons finely chopped fresh cilantro

3 tablespoons finely chopped fresh mint leaves

freshly ground black pepper

Serves 4

Baking en papillote *is one of the easiest and healthiest ways of cooking fish. The fish and vegetables are laid on a large piece of foil, flavored with a splash of wine, a knob of butter, and some fresh herbs, then tightly sealed so that they steam in their own juices. Light and delicious.*

sea bass en papillote
with spring vegetables & fresh herbs

8 oz. mixed vegetables, such as asparagus, broccoli, zucchini, sugarsnap peas, green beans, or baby carrots

light olive oil, for greasing

2 thick sea bass fillets, about 4¹/₂ oz. each

2 teaspoons mixed fresh herbs, such as chives, chervil, and dill

1¹/₂ tablespoons butter, cut into slices

4 tablespoons dry white wine, such as Pinot Grigio or Sauvignon Blanc

sea salt and freshly ground black pepper

4 large pieces of foil or parchment paper, about 11 inches square

a baking tray

Serves 2

Chop the vegetables into large, even-sized pieces. Lay out 2 pieces of foil or parchment paper one on top of the other and grease the top layer lightly with a few drops of olive oil. Lay 1 seabass fillet on top of the foil or paper and surround it with half the vegetables. Sprinkle with half the herbs, dot with half the butter, and season with salt and pepper. Pull up the sides of the foil or parchment paper and add 2 tablespoons wine to the package. Carefully pull the sides together around the fish and vegetables, leaving a space around them, but sealing the package tightly at the top so the juices can't escape. Repeat to make a second package.

Put the 2 packages on a baking tray and bake in a preheated oven at 425°F for 12 minutes. Remove the packages from the oven and open them carefully. Transfer the fish and vegetables to 2 warm plates, pour over the juices, and serve immediately.

Recommended wine match A classic French wine, such as Chablis or Sancerre would respect the delicate flavors of this dish. Or try a Spanish Albariño.

Monkfish makes an excellent alternative to a meaty roast, especially when it is served with a robust red wine gravy. It also makes an impressive entrée for a dinner party. You can prepare the monkfish yourself, but to make life easier ask your fishmonger to do it for you.

roast monkfish

with pancetta, rosemary, & **red wine gravy**

Strip the leaves from 4 of the rosemary sprigs, chop them very finely, and transfer to a bowl. Crush 1 garlic clove and add it to the rosemary along with the softened butter. Season with a little salt and pepper and beat well with a wooden spoon.

Lay out the monkfish fillets in pairs with the thin end of 1 fillet next to the thick end of the other. Spread the rosemary and garlic butter over one side of each fillet, then press each pair together with the buttered sides in the middle. Wrap the slices of pancetta or bacon around each pair of fillets, enclosing them completely. Put 1 tablespoon olive oil in a shallow cast-iron pan (or another dish that you can later put on the burner), then add the wrapped monkfish. Put the remaining garlic cloves, rosemary sprigs, and the shallots around the monkfish, then drizzle over the remaining oil. Roast in a preheated oven at 400°F for 25 minutes, turning the shallots and garlic halfway through, until the pancetta or bacon is nicely browned.

Carefully remove the monkfish from the pan, lightly cover it with foil, and set aside. Leaving the shallots and garlic in the pan, pour off all but 1 tablespoon of the oil and butter, then put the pan over medium heat. Heat the contents of the pan for a couple of minutes, stirring, then pour in the wine. Let it bubble up and reduce by half, then add the broth. Continue to let it bubble until the liquid is reduced by half again. Strain the gravy through a fine-meshed sieve and return it to the pan, along with any juices that have accumulated from the fish. Reheat gently, then beat in the chilled butter. Check the seasoning—it may need a little pepper, but probably no more salt.

Cut the monkfish fillets into thick slices, divide them between 4 or 6 plates, and spoon over a little red wine gravy. Serve with sautéed potatoes and mixed salad greens.

Recommended wine match I'd suggest a Merlot or a Sangiovese or Sangiovese-based Italian red with this dish.

---

8 sprigs of rosemary

7 garlic cloves

4 tablespoons butter at room temperature, plus an extra 2 tablespoons, chilled and cut into cubes

2 small monkfish tails, about 1 lb. each, skinned, boned, and each divided into 2 fillets

4 oz. very thinly sliced pancetta or bacon, rind removed

2 tablespoons olive oil

8 shallots, quartered

3/4 cup full-bodied fruity red wine, such as Merlot or Argentinian Malbec

1/2 cup light chicken or vegetable broth

sea salt and freshly ground black pepper

To serve

sautéed potatoes

mixed salad greens

Serves 4–6

poultry

This is one of the easiest supper dishes imaginable. It takes less time to cook than a supermarket ready meal, and it is much more delicious. You can use any dry white wine to make it, but I particularly like the richness of Viognier, an exotic, slightly scented grape variety that thrives in southern France and, nowadays, in California, too. Unoaked or lightly oaked Chardonnay will also work well.

sautéed chicken

with **white wine**, pea, & tarragon sauce

1 tablespoon olive oil

3½ oz. pancetta or lean bacon, chopped

2 skinless, boneless chicken breasts, cut into thin slices

1 small onion, very finely chopped

⅔ cup full-bodied dry white wine, such as Viognier

1 cup fresh or frozen peas

2 tablespoons finely chopped fresh tarragon leaves

about 4 generous tablespoons sour cream or crème fraîche

freshly ground black pepper

steamed asparagus tips, to serve

Serves 2

Heat the oil in a large skillet, then add the pancetta or bacon. Fry for a couple of minutes until the fat starts to run. Add the chicken slices and fry, stirring occasionally, until lightly golden, 4 to 5 minutes.

Add the onion to the pan and fry for 1 to 2 minutes. Add the wine and peas and cook until the wine has reduced by about two-thirds. Reduce the heat and stir in the tarragon, sour cream or crème fraîche, and black pepper, to taste. Heat gently until almost bubbling.

Remove the pan from the heat. Transfer the sautéed chicken to 2 warm plates, spoon over the sauce, and serve immediately with steamed asparagus tips.

Recommended wine match Serve a glass of the wine used to make the dish—a Viognier or an unoaked or lightly oaked Chardonnay.

This dish is perfect for a romantic dinner for two, therefore it's worth using a really good wine to make it. You need only a glass for cooking the chicken, so the rest of the bottle can be drunk with the meal.

chicken
with **chardonnay** & chanterelles

Put the chanterelles in a bowl and add just enough tepid water to cover. Let soak for 10 minutes. Drain the chanterelles, reserve the soaking liquid, and strain it through a fine sieve.

Put the flour in a shallow dish and season it with salt and pepper. Dip the chicken breasts in the flour and coat both sides. Heat a skillet over moderate heat, add 1 tablespoon olive oil and 1 tablespoon butter. When the butter is foaming, add the chicken breasts skin side down. Fry for $2^1/_2$ to 3 minutes until the skin is brown and crisp. Turn the chicken breasts over and lightly brown the other side, $2^1/_2$ to 3 minutes. Transfer the chicken to an ovenproof dish and cook in a preheated oven at 400°F for 20 minutes until cooked.

Meanwhile, discard the fat from the skillet and wipe it with paper towels. Heat the remaining oil and 1 tablespoon butter in the skillet, add the shallots, and sauté gently for 5 to 6 minutes or until soft. Stir in the paprika, then increase the heat to high and add the wine. When the wine has reduced by half, add $1/_3$ cup of the reserved mushroom water. Reduce the heat and let simmer gently for 10 minutes. Strain the sauce through a fine sieve into a heatproof bowl. Return the strained sauce to the pan, add the chanterelles, cover, and let simmer for 10 minutes.

Remove the pan from the heat, stir in the cream, and salt and pepper to taste. Return the pan to the burner and heat very gently, stirring occasionally, until the sauce thickens.

To cook the pasta, bring a large saucepan of lightly salted water to the boil, add the pasta, and cook until *al dente*, according to the instructions on the package. Drain well, add 1 tablespoon butter, and season with a little pepper and freshly grated nutmeg.

Cut each chicken breast into 5 or 6 thick diagonal slices. Divide the pasta between 2 warm plates, put the slices of chicken on top, then spoon over the mushroom and cream sauce. Sprinkle with chopped parsley and serve immediately.

$^1/_2$ **oz. dried chanterelles**

1 tablespoon flour

2 boneless chicken breasts, about 12 oz.

2 tablespoons olive oil

3 tablespoons butter

4 shallots, thinly sliced

a good pinch of Spanish sweet smoked paprika (pimentòn)

$^2/_3$ **cup top quality New World Chardonnay or good white Burgundy**

3 tablespoons heavy cream

2 coils dried *pappardelle all'uovo* or other wide-ribboned egg pasta, about $3^1/_2$ oz.

freshly grated nutmeg

1 tablespoon finely chopped fresh parsley

sea salt and freshly ground black pepper

an ovenproof dish

Serves 2

This classic French recipe is a terrific dish for a dinner party because it tastes even better the day after it's made, so you can prepare it ahead. The French would always use a local wine to make it—I'd suggest a good Côtes du Rhône-Villages, a Gigondas, or a fruity young Syrah.

coq au vin

10 oz. shallots

3 tablespoons flour

6 large skinless, boneless chicken breasts

3 tablespoons olive oil

4 oz. chopped bacon or pancetta

2 garlic cloves, thinly sliced

¹⁄₄ cup brandy

3 sprigs of fresh thyme

1 bay leaf

1 bottle dry fruity red wine (see recipe introduction), 750 ml

8 oz. small button mushrooms

1 tablespoon butter, softened (optional)

¹⁄₄ cup chopped fresh flat-leaf parsley

sea salt and freshly ground black pepper

creamy mashed potatoes or tagliatelle, to serve

Serves 6

Cut the shallots into even-sized pieces, leaving the small ones whole and cutting the others in half or quarters.

Put 2 tablespoons flour in a shallow dish and season it with salt and pepper. Dip the chicken breasts in the flour and coat both sides. Heat 2 tablespoons olive oil in a large lidded skillet or deep casserole, add the chicken breasts, and fry for 2 to 3 minutes on each side until lightly browned—you may have to do this in 2 batches.

Remove the chicken from the pan, discard the oil, and wipe the pan with paper towels. Return the pan to the heat and pour in the remaining oil. Add the chopped bacon or pancetta and the shallots and fry until lightly browned. Stir in the garlic, then return the chicken to the pan. Put the brandy in a small saucepan and heat it until almost boiling. Set it alight with a long kitchen match and carefully pour it over the chicken. Let the flames die down, then add the thyme and bay leaf and pour in enough wine to just cover the chicken. Bring back to simmering point, then reduce the heat, half cover the pan, and simmer very gently for 45 minutes. (If you're making this dish ahead of time, take the pan off the heat after 30 minutes, let cool, and refrigerate overnight.) Add the mushrooms to the pan and cook for another 10 to 15 minutes.

Remove the chicken from the pan, set aside, and keep it warm. Using a slotted spoon, scoop the shallots, bacon pieces or pancetta cubes, and mushrooms out of the pan and keep them warm. Increase the heat under the pan and let the sauce simmer until it has reduced by half. If the sauce needs thickening, mash 1 tablespoon soft butter with 1 tablespoon flour to give a smooth paste, then add it bit by bit to the sauce, beating well after each addition, until the sauce is smooth and glossy.

Return the shallots, pancetta, and mushrooms to the pan. Check the seasoning and add salt and pepper, to taste. Cut each chicken breast into 4 slices and arrange them on warm serving plates. Spoon a generous amount of sauce over the chicken and sprinkle with parsley. Serve with creamy mashed potatoes or tagliatelle.

Red wine and cinnamon are natural partners and work together brilliantly in this exotically spiced, Moorish-style casserole. I suggest you use a really strong, fruity wine such as a Merlot, Carmenère, or Zinfandel.

duck casserole

with **red wine**, cinnamon, & olives

Trim any excess fat from all the duck pieces and prick the skin with a fork. Cut the breasts in half lengthwise and season all the pieces lightly with salt and pepper. Put 1 tablespoon oil in an ovenproof dish and add the duck pieces, skin side upward. Roast in a preheated oven at 400°F for 20 minutes, then remove from the oven and pour off the fat (keep it for roasting potatoes). Reduce the oven temperature to 300°F.

Meanwhile, heat the remaining oil in a flameproof casserole, add the onion and celery, and sauté over low heat for 5 to 6 minutes or until soft. Stir in the garlic, increase the heat, and pour in the red wine. Simmer for 1 to 2 minutes, then add the strained tomatoes, orange zest, cinnamon, olives, and herbs. Transfer the duck pieces to the casserole and spoon the sauce over them. Bring the sauce to a simmer, cover, and transfer the casserole to the preheated oven for about 1¼ hours until the duck is tender. Spoon the sauce over the duck halfway through cooking—add a little water if the sauce seems too dry.

Take the casserole out of the oven, remove and discard the cinnamon stick and orange zest, and spoon off any fat that has accumulated on the surface. Stir in 2 tablespoons red wine and season to taste with salt and pepper.

Serve with couscous or a lightly spiced pilaf or with *cavolo nero* or other dark leafy greens.

Note You can also make this casserole a day ahead. To do so, cook it in the oven for just 1 hour, then let it cool, cover, and refrigerate overnight. The following day, skim off any fat, then reheat it gently, adding a final dash of wine just before serving.

Recommended wine match Any robust southern French, Spanish, Portuguese, or southern Italian red would go well with this recipe. As would a good, gutsy Zinfandel.

---

2 duck breasts

4 duck legs

3 tablespoons olive oil

1 medium onion, thinly sliced

1 celery stalk, thinly sliced

1 garlic clove, crushed

1½ cups full-bodied fruity red wine (see recipe introduction), plus 2 tablespoons extra

1 cup strained tomatoes

2 small strips of unwaxed orange zest

1 cinnamon stick

⅔ cup pitted mixed olives marinated with herbs

½ teaspoon *herbes de Provence* or dried oregano

sea salt and freshly ground black pepper

To serve, your choice of:

couscous

pilaf

leafy green vegetables, such as *cavolo nero*

an ovenproof dish

Serves 4

meat

This typical wine, cream, and mustard sauce from Burgundy is quick, easy, and versatile. You could equally well use it for chicken.

burgundy-style pork
with **white wine** & mustard sauce

Heat the oil and butter in a medium skillet. Add the pork chops and brown them for about 3 minutes on each side. Reduce the heat and cook for a further 2 to 3 minutes on each side or until cooked. Remove the pork chops from the pan, set aside, and keep them warm.

Add the mushrooms to the pan and cook until lightly browned, about 5 minutes. Scoop them out with a slotted spoon, add to the pork, and keep warm. Using a wooden spoon, stir the flour into the juices in the pan. Stir in the wine and thyme leaves and let bubble up until reduced by about two-thirds. Reduce the heat to very low, then stir in the sour cream or crème fraîche and mustard. Heat very gently, taking care not to let the sauce boil or the mustard will taste bitter. Season to taste with salt and pepper.

Return the pork, mushrooms, and any juices to the pan and heat through very gently. To serve, put the pork steaks on 2 warm plates, spoon the sauce over the top, sprinkle with a few snipped chives, and accompany with new potatoes and a salad greens.

Recommended wine match Chablis would go very well with this dish, as would a young, red Burgundy.

1 tablespoon olive oil

1$\frac{1}{2}$ tablespoons butter

2 boneless pork loin chops, about 10 oz. in total

4 oz. cremini mushrooms, rinsed and thickly sliced

1 teaspoon flour

$\frac{1}{2}$ cup (100 ml) white Burgundy or other dry white wine

1 teaspoon chopped fresh thyme leaves

2 tablespoons sour cream or crème fraîche

2 rounded teaspoons whole-grain Dijon mustard or other whole-grain mustard

sea salt and freshly ground black pepper

To serve

1 tablespoon snipped fresh chives

boiled new potatoes

salad greens

Serves 2

This is one of my favorite family recipes for the weekend. You can leave it for hours gently bubbling away in the oven and you will have a fantastic dish at the end of the day. I generally use an Italian wine like a Pinot Grigio, but you could use any dry white wine.

italian-style roast pork
with **white wine**, garlic, & fennel

6¹/₂ **lb. boned, rolled shoulder of pork**

2 **tablespoons fennel seeds**

1 **tablespoon coarse sea salt**

1 **teaspoon black peppercorns**

1 **teaspoon crushed dried chiles**

6 **large garlic cloves, roughly chopped**

freshly squeezed juice of 2 lemons

2 **tablespoons olive oil**

³/₄ **cup dry white wine**

To serve, your choice of:

sautéed potatoes and salad

mashed potatoes and green beans

a large roasting pan with a rack

an ovenproof dish

Serves 8

Cut deep slits in the roast with a sharp knife. Grind the fennel seeds, salt, peppercorns, and chiles using a pestle and mortar. Add the chopped garlic and pound to a rough paste. Using your hands, smother the paste all over the pork working it into the slits. Put the pork on a wire rack and place it over a roasting pan. Cook, skin side up in a preheated oven at 450°F for 30 minutes. Remove the pork from the oven and reduce the heat to 225°F.

Turn the pork over and pour half the lemon juice and all of the olive oil over it. Return the pork to the oven and cook for at least 7 hours, checking it every couple of hours. You should be aware that the meat is cooking—it should be sizzling quietly. Ovens vary, so you may want to increase the temperature slightly.

About halfway through the cooking time, spoon off the excess fat and squeeze the remaining lemon juice over the meat. About 30 minutes before the pork is due to be cooked, remove it from the oven and increase the heat to 425°F. Transfer the pork, fat side up, to a clean ovenproof dish and when the oven is hot, return the pork to the oven for 15 to 20 minutes to crisp up the crackling. Remove from the oven and let rest.

Pour off any excess fat from the original roasting pan and add the wine and ³/₄ cup water. Heat gently on the top of the stove, working off any sticky burnt-on bits from the edges of the pan, and simmer for 10 minutes. Strain the juices through a sieve and keep them warm.

Carve the pork into thick slices. Put a few slices on each of 8 warmed plates and pour some of the pan juices over the top. You could serve this with sautéed potatoes and salad, or mashed potatoes and green beans.

Recommended wine match If you want to stick to white, a quality Pinot Grigio or Italian Soave would be perfect with this dish. Or try a Chianti Classico.

This is a really robust pasta dish that's perfect to serve in cold weather. The wine gives a richer, more warming flavor than the usual tomato-based sauce.

rigatoni

with eggplant, sausage, & zinfandel sauce

12 oz. fresh Italian sausages

4 tablespoons olive oil

1 medium eggplant, cut into cubes

1 medium onion, finely chopped

1 red bell pepper, seeded and cut into 1-inch pieces

1 rounded tablespoon tomato purée

2 garlic cloves, crushed

1 teaspoon dried oregano

³/₄ cup Zinfandel or other full-bodied, fruity red wine

³/₄ cup fresh chicken broth, or light vegetable broth made from 1 teaspoon vegetable bouillon powder

12 oz. dried pasta tubes, such as rigatoni or penne

4 tablespoons chopped fresh parsley

sea salt and freshly ground black pepper

Serves 4

Slit the sausage skins with a sharp knife, peel them off, and discard. Roughly chop the sausage meat. Heat 1 tablespoon olive oil in a large skillet or wok, add the sausage meat, breaking it up with a spatula or wooden spoon, and sauté until lightly golden. Using a slotted spoon, remove the meat from the pan and set aside.

Add 2 more tablespoons oil to the pan, add the eggplant, and stir fry for 3 to 4 minutes until it starts to brown. Add the remaining oil and the chopped onion and sauté for 1 to 2 minutes. Add the red pepper and sauté for 1 to 2 minutes more. Return the sausage meat to the pan, stir in the tomato purée, and cook for 1 minute. Add the garlic, oregano, and wine and simmer until the wine has reduced by half. Stir in the broth and let simmer over low heat for about 10 minutes.

Meanwhile, to cook the pasta, bring a large saucepan of lightly salted water to a boil. Add the pasta and cook for about 10 minutes until *al dente*, or according to the instructions on the package. When the pasta is just cooked, spoon off a couple of tablespoons of the cooking water and stir it into the wine sauce. Drain the pasta thoroughly, then tip it into the sauce. Add 3 tablespoons parsley and mix well. Remove the pan from the heat, cover, and let stand for 2 to 3 minutes for the flavors to meld.

Check the seasoning, adding salt and pepper to taste, then spoon the pasta and sauce into 4 warm serving bowls. Serve immediately, sprinkled with the remaining parsley.

Recommended wine match A Zinfandel would be the obvious choice, but any robust medium- to full-bodied red would work well.

Believe it or not, the preparation and cooking of this dish can be spread over three days, which makes it the perfect dish to serve for Sunday lunch. Start marinating the meat on Friday evening, cook it on Saturday, then simply reheat it on Sunday. The initial marinating gives the meat a fantastically rich flavor.

slow braised lamb shanks
with **red wine**, rosemary, & garlic

Put the lamb shanks in a large, heavyweight plastic bag. Add the onion, carrots, garlic, rosemary, and peppercorns. Pour in the bottle of wine, then pull up the sides of the bag so the marinade covers the meat. Secure the top of the bag with a wire twist. Put the bag in a bowl or dish and refrigerate overnight.

The next day, remove the lamb shanks from the marinade, pat them dry with paper towels, and season with salt and pepper. Strain the marinade through a sieve into a large bowl and reserve the vegetables.

Heat half the oil in a large flameproof casserole, add the lamb shanks, and brown them thoroughly on all sides—you may need to do this in 2 batches. Remove the lamb and set it aside. Add the remaining oil to the casserole, then add the reserved vegetables and sauté briefly until they begin to soften. Add a few tablespoons of the marinade and let it bubble up, incorporating any caramelized juices that have stuck to the casserole. Stir in the strained tomatoes and the rest of the marinade, then return the lamb shanks to the pan. Spoon the vegetables and sauce over the lamb and bring to simmering point. Cover the meat tightly with wax paper or parchment paper, put the lid on the casserole, and cook in a preheated oven at 325°F for $1^{3}/_{4}$ to 2 hours until the meat is almost tender.

Remove the lid and paper and cook for a further 30 minutes. Remove the rosemary sprigs, let cool, cover, and refrigerate overnight.

The next day, carefully remove any fat that has accumulated on the surface. Reheat gently on the top of the stove until the sauce comes to simmering point. If the sauce isn't thick enough, remove the lamb shanks from the pan, simmer the sauce until it thickens, then return the lamb to the pan. Add the remaining glass of wine and simmer for a further 15 minutes. Season to taste with salt and pepper and sweeten with a little tomato ketchup, if necessary. Serve with creamy mashed potatoes.

6 even-sized lamb shanks, about $4^{1}/_{2}$ lb. in total

1 large onion, thinly sliced

3 carrots, cut into thin sticks

4 garlic cloves, thinly sliced

2–3 sprigs of rosemary

$^{1}/_{2}$ teaspoon black peppercorns

1 bottle robust red wine, 750 ml, such as Shiraz, Malbec, or Zinfandel, plus $^{1}/_{2}$ cup extra to finish

4 tablespoons olive oil

2 cups strained tomatoes

tomato ketchup, to taste

sea salt and freshly ground black pepper

creamy mashed potatoes, to serve

a large heavyweight plastic bag

a lidded flameproof casserole, preferably large enough to hold the shanks in a single layer

Serves 6

4 large veal chops,
about 2¼ lb. in total

2 tablespoons olive oil

1 tablespoon butter

1 small onion, finely chopped

1 celery stalk, thinly sliced

2 garlic cloves, crushed

²/₃ cup Italian dry white wine,
such as Pinot Grigio

²/₃ cup strained tomatoes

about 1¼ cups light vegetable
or chicken broth

Green olive gremolata

finely grated zest of
1 unwaxed lemon

10 pitted green olives,
finely chopped

3 heaped tablespoons finely
chopped fresh parsley

To serve, your choice of:

saffron risotto

plain boiled rice

green salad

Serves 4

Osso buco is one of those dishes about which huge arguments rage. Whether there should be tomato or no tomato. At what stage you should add the gremolata (the parsley, lemon, and garlic topping). Whether it should be cooked for one hour or three. The only thing Italians seem to be able to agree on is that it should contain veal and white wine. Well, this version gives the dish a complete makeover. It's fresher, faster, but just as delicious.

osso buco-style veal chops
with green olive gremolata

Trim any excess fat from the chops. Heat a large, shallow skillet, then add the oil and heat for 1 minute. Add the butter and, when the foaming has subsided, add the veal chops and sauté them for about 3 minutes on each side until nicely browned. Remove the chops and set aside.

Add the onion and celery to the skillet and cook over low heat for 5 to 6 minutes until softened. Stir in the garlic, then increase the heat to high and pour in the wine. Let it bubble up for a few minutes until the wine has reduced by half, then add the strained tomatoes and 1 cup of the broth. Stir well, then return the chops to the skillet, spooning the sauce over them. Bring the sauce back to a simmer, half cover the skillet, and reduce the heat. Cook very gently for about 40 minutes, turning the chops halfway through, until they are tender. If they seem to be getting dry, add a little more broth.

Meanwhile, to prepare the gremolata, put the lemon zest, olives, and parsley in a bowl and mix well. When the chops are ready, add half the gremolata to the skillet and stir to mix. Cook over very low heat for 5 minutes for the flavors to meld.

Transfer the chops to 4 warm plates, spoon the sauce over the top, and sprinkle with the remaining gremolata. Serve with a saffron risotto, plain boiled rice, or a simple green salad.

Recommended wine match I'd personally drink a dry Italian white with this, such as an Orvieto or Verdicchio dei Castelli de Jesi, but you could opt for an Italian red—a Barbera, for example.

This has to be the ultimate fast-food recipe. You can make it from start to finish in 5 minutes. The red wine gives a wonderful instant sauce that takes the dish into the luxury league. After you have made this a couple of times, you'll find you won't need measurements—just pour in a dash of brandy, half a glass of red wine, and a slosh of cream to finish, and away you go.

pepper-crusted steaks
with **red wine** sauce

Put the peppercorns and salt in a mortar and pound with a pestle until coarsely ground. Tip into a shallow dish and mix in the flour. Dip each steak into the pepper mixture and press the coating in lightly, turning to coat both sides.

Heat a skillet over medium heat and add the oil and half the butter. Once the butter has melted, add the steaks, and cook for 1 1/2 minutes. Turn them over and cook for 30 seconds on the other side. Transfer the steaks to 2 warm plates.

Pour the brandy into the pan and light it carefully with a long cook's match or taper. When the flames die down, add the wine and cook for a few seconds. Add the broth and simmer for 1 to 2 minutes. Sweeten with a little red currant jelly or balsamic vinegar, if liked, then stir in the sour cream or crème fraîche.

Pour the sauce over the steaks and serve with an arugula salad and some crusty bread. If you're not in a hurry, this also goes really well with garlic mashed potatoes.

Recommended wine match This is the kind of dish that will take almost any medium- to full-bodied red, such as a Merlot, a Cabernet Sauvignon, or a Shiraz.

1 tablespoon mixed peppercorns

1/2 teaspoon sea salt

1 teaspoon flour

2 thinly cut rump steaks, about 5 oz. each, fat removed

1 tablespoon olive oil

2 tablespoons butter

2 tablespoons brandy

1/3 cup full-bodied fruity red wine, such as Zinfandel, Merlot, or Cabernet Sauvignon

3 tablespoons fresh beef or chicken broth

1 teaspoon red currant jelly or a few drops of balsamic vinegar (optional)

2 tablespoons sour cream or crème fraîche

To serve, your choice of:

arugula salad and crusty bread

garlic mashed potatoes

Serves 2

2¼ lb. thickly sliced braising or stewing beef

2 tablespoons flour

5–6 tablespoons olive oil

1 large onion, thinly sliced

2 large garlic cloves, crushed

1 tablespoon tomato purée

1¼ cups Faugères or other full-bodied fruity red

½ cup homemade or organic beef broth

1 teaspoon *herbes de Provence*

1 thin strip of unwaxed orange zest

2 bay leaves

⅔ cup black olives

3 heaped tablespoons roughly chopped flat-leaf parsley

sea salt and freshly ground black pepper

Slow-roasted carrots

1 lb. carrots

a pinch of cayenne pepper

2 tablespoons olive oil

a cast-iron casserole

a large ovenproof dish

Serves 4–6

This adaptation of the classic French daube is one of my favorite dishes to make at our holiday home in France. Of course I use the delicious local red Faugères wine, but you could use any robust fruity red. Note that I add a little extra wine right at the end—it lifts the winey flavor after the long, slow cooking. I also like to keep the carrots separate because they look so lovely and colorful and they taste more intense if you cook them on their own.

languedoc beef stew
with **red wine**, herbs, & olives

Trim any excess fat from the beef, then cut the meat into large cubes. Put the flour in a shallow dish and season it with salt and pepper. Dip the cubes of beef in the flour to coat.

Heat 2 tablespoons oil in a large skillet, add the beef, and sauté on all sides until the meat is browned—you will need to do this in batches, adding extra oil as you go. Transfer the beef to a cast-iron casserole.

Heat the remaining oil in the skillet, add the onion, and cook for 3 to 4 minutes until softened but not browned. Add the garlic and tomato purée and cook for 1 minute, stirring. Add 1 cup of the wine, the broth, *herbes de Provence*, orange zest, and bay leaves. Bring to a boil, then pour the sauce into the casserole. Heat the casserole over medium heat and bring the sauce back to a boil. Reduce the heat, cover, and simmer very gently for 2½ to 3 hours until the meat is completely tender. Check the contents of the casserole occasionally to ensure there is enough liquid (add a little extra broth or water if it's dry).

About two-thirds of the way through the cooking time, prepare the slow-roasted carrots. Cut the carrots into long, thick diagonal slices. Put the carrots, salt, and cayenne pepper in a large, shallow ovenproof dish, pour the oil over, and toss well. Bake in a preheated oven at 350°F for 45 to 60 minutes until the carrots are soft and their edges are caramelized.

About 30 minutes before the stew should be ready, stir in the olives. Just before serving, season to taste with salt and pepper, then stir in the parsley and the remaining wine, and cook for a further 5 minutes. Serve with the slow-roasted carrots.

Recommended wine match Try a Faugères or other full-bodied Languedoc red.

sweet things & drinks

If you were going to serve fresh fruit in wine, you would think that it would need to be a sweet wine, but strangely enough it can work equally well with a dry one—especially Italy's fashionable sparkler, prosecco. The secret ingredient in this recipe is the peach schnapps, which subtly enhances the peach flavor.

peaches in prosecco

Cut the peaches in half by cutting vertically around the fruit with a sharp knife, then twisting the 2 halves in opposite directions. Cut each half into 2 pieces and peel off the skin. Cut each piece into 3 slices and transfer them to a deep bowl. Sprinkle over the lemon juice and mix gently (this will stop them discoloring). Pour over the peach schnapps or peach-flavored liqueur and about two-thirds of the chilled prosecco. Cover the bowl with plastic wrap and chill in the refrigerator for about 1 hour to let the flavors blend. Keep the remaining prosecco in the refrigerator.

Before serving, taste for sweetness and add an extra splash of peach schnapps, if necessary. To serve, arrange the peach slices in 6 individual glass dishes and layer a few raspberries in between. Ladle the peach schnapps and prosecco over the fruit, then top up with more prosecco to cover the fruit, if necessary. I prefer to serve this on its own, but you could offer some light cream, if you like.

4 large ripe peaches

1 tablespoon freshly squeezed lemon juice

3/4 cup peach schnapps or peach-flavored liqueur

1 bottle prosecco, 750 ml, chilled

1 cup raspberries

light cream, to serve (optional)

6 individual glass dishes

Serves 6

Roasting pears in wine transforms them from everyday fruit into a light but luxurious dinner party dessert. Their gentle flavor makes a perfect foil for a fine dessert wine. The trick is to use an inexpensive wine for cooking and a better wine of the same type to serve with it.

roasted pears

with **sweet wine**, honey, & pine nuts

freshly squeezed juice of
1 large lemon

9 medium just-ripe Anjou pears

4 tablespoons butter, softened

3 tablespoons fragrant honey,
such as orange blossom

³/₄ cup Premières Côtes de
Bordeaux or a late harvested
Sauvignon or Semillon

¹/₃ cup pine nuts

2 teaspoons sugar

³/₄ cup heavy cream

2 teaspoons vanilla sugar or
¹/₂ teaspoon pure vanilla extract
mixed with 2 teaspoons sugar

*a large ovenproof dish, buttered
(large enough to hold the pears
in a single layer)*

Serves 6

Strain the lemon juice into a small bowl. Cut the pears in half, peel them, and remove the cores. Dip the pear halves in the lemon juice (this will prevent them discoloring), then put them, cut sides upward, in the prepared ovenproof dish. Make sure the pears fit snugly in one layer. Put a small knob of butter in the hollow of each pear, then drizzle them with the honey, wine, and any remaining lemon juice.

Bake in a preheated oven at 375°F for 50 to 60 minutes, turning the pears over halfway through. If you notice while the pears are cooking that they are producing a lot of juice, increase the oven temperature to 400°F to concentrate the juices and form a syrup. Remove the pears from the oven and let cool for about 20 minutes.

Meanwhile, lightly toast the pine nuts in a dry, nonstick skillet, shaking the pan occasionally, until they start to brown. Sprinkle over the sugar and continue to cook until the sugar melts and caramelizes. Put the cream and vanilla sugar in a small saucepan and heat gently, stirring occasionally, until lukewarm.

To serve, put 3 pear halves on each plate, trickle over 1 tablespoon warm cream, and scatter over a few caramelized pine nuts. Alternatively, serve the cream separately for your guests to pour over.

Recommended wine match This is a good dessert to pair with a Sauternes or another sweet, Bordeaux-style wine.

With so many excellent ice creams available to buy, it might seem unnecessary to make your own, but I promise you this homemade version is worth the effort.

red wine & cherry ripple ice cream

To make the cherry sauce, put the cherries, raspberries, and 3 tablespoons sugar in a saucepan. Heat gently, stirring occasionally, until the sugar has dissolved. Add ¹/₃ cup wine, bring to a boil, and simmer for 10 to 15 minutes until the cherries are soft and the liquid is syrupy. Taste and add extra sugar, if necessary. Let cool, then chill in the refrigerator.

Put the egg yolks and ¹/₂ cup sugar in a heatproof bowl and beat with a hand-held electric mixer until smooth, pale, and moussey. Put the cream, milk, and remaining sugar in a saucepan and heat gently until almost boiling. Pour the hot cream in a steady stream over the egg mixture, beating constantly until smooth.

Pour the custard through a fine-mesh sieve back into the rinsed pan. Heat very gently, stirring constantly with a wooden spoon, until the custard thickens and coats the back of the spoon. If it looks like it's starting to boil, remove the pan from the heat and stir for a couple of minutes to let cool slightly before returning it to the burner. Stir in the vanilla extract, then let the custard cool completely.

Pour the cold custard into a plastic container and freeze. Remove it from the freezer after about 1 hour when the edges have begun to harden. Beat with a hand held electric mixer. Return to the freezer, then beat again after 30 minutes. (Or churn in an ice cream maker.)

When the mixture is the consistency of soft scoop ice cream, take half the cherry mixture and cut up any larger pieces of fruit. Put a few teaspoons of the mixture into the ice cream, dragging the fruit through it with the point of a skewer. Carefully turn the ice cream over with a tablespoon and repeat until this half of the cherry mixture has been used. Freeze the ice cream for several hours and refrigerate the rest of the sauce.

Transfer the ice cream to the refrigerator for 15 to 20 minutes to soften slightly before serving. Meanwhile, put the remaining cherry mixture, the remaining wine, and a splash of kirsch or cherry brandy, if using, in a saucepan and heat gently until almost boiling. Let cool for 10 minutes. Serve the ice cream in scoops with the warm cherry sauce poured over.

6 extra-large egg yolks

¹/₂ cup plus 3 tablespoons granulated sugar

2 cups light cream

2 tablespoons whole milk

1 teaspoon pure vanilla extract

Cherry sauce

1³/₄ cups pitted dark red cherries or a large jar of morello cherries, drained

1 cup fresh or frozen raspberries

3–4 tablespoons sugar

¹/₂ cup fruity red wine, such as Merlot

1 tablespoon Kirsch or cherry brandy (optional)

an ice cream maker (optional)

Serves 4–6

Syllabub—a velvety-smooth concoction of sweet wine and cream—is one of the great English desserts, dating from the 16th century. I like it, for a change, made with orange rather than lemon and topped with what my daughter calls "orange sprinkle," an irresistibly crunchy mixture of orange zest and sugar.

orange syllabub
with crunchy orange sprinkle

²/₃ **cup southern French Muscat or other strong sweet white wine (15 percent ABV)**

1 tablespoon Cointreau or other orange liqueur

finely grated zest of 2 unwaxed oranges

2 tablespoons freshly squeezed orange juice

2 tablespoons freshly squeezed lemon juice

4 tablespoons sugar

1³/₄ **cup heavy cream, chilled**

1 large bowl, chilled for 30–40 minutes in the refrigerator

6 glass dishes

Serves 6

Pour the wine into a bowl, add the Cointreau or orange liqueur, half the grated orange zest, the orange and lemon juice, and 2 tablespoons sugar. Stir, cover, and chill in the refrigerator for several hours or overnight.

Mix the remaining orange zest and sugar in a bowl. Spread it over a plate and leave for a couple of hours to crisp up. Store it in an airtight container until ready to serve.

Strain the wine mixture through a fine, non-metallic sieve. Pour the cream into the large chilled bowl and beat with a hand-held electric mixer until it starts to thicken. Gradually add the orange-flavored wine, beating well after each addition, until the cream thickens again—you want a thick pouring consistency. When the final addition of wine has been incorporated the mixture should hold a trail when you lift out the beaters, but it shouldn't be stiff. (Don't overbeat it, or it will separate.) Ladle the mixture into 6 individual glass dishes and chill them in the refrigerator for at least 1 hour before serving.

Just before serving, sprinkle the orange sugar over the top of each syllabub.

Recommended wine match I don't think you need to serve wine with this syllabub, but a small glass of well-chilled Sauternes or late-harvested or botrytized Sauvignon or Sémillon would go well.

Wine and fruit make fabulously pretty fruit jellies that offer a refreshing end to a dinner party. You don't have to use a sweet wine, although the aromatized wine I've used in the variation—the sparkling nectarine and blueberry jellies— works really well. Just add sugar syrup to taste.

sparkling shiraz & summer berry jellies

Put the gelatin in a flat dish and sprinkle over 3 tablespoons cold water. Let soak for 3 minutes until soft, then drain off the water. Heat the sparkling wine in a saucepan until hot but not boiling. Tip the soaked gelatin into the wine and stir until dissolved. Set aside and let cool.

Rinse the berries, then put them in a shallow bowl. Cut the strawberries in half or quarters, depending on their size. Sprinkle over 1 to 2 tablespoons sugar and set aside to macerate.

Check the liquid jelly for sweetness and add sugar syrup to taste. Put an assortment of berries in the bottom of 6 glasses or glass dishes and pour over enough jelly to cover them. Put the jellies in the refrigerator and let set, 45 to 60 minutes. Add the remaining fruit to the glasses and top with the remaining jelly. (If the jelly in the saucepan has started to set, reheat it very gently, stirring, until smooth and liquid, then let cool before pouring it over the fruit.) Return the jellies to the refrigerator for another 45 to 60 minutes until set. Serve with cream or vanilla ice cream.

Note To make the sugar syrup, put $^1/_2$ cup sugar and $^2/_3$ cup water in a saucepan and heat gently until the sugar has dissolved. Bring to a boil and simmer for 3 to 4 minutes. You can use the syrup immediately or let it cool and store it in the refrigerator for up to 2 weeks.

Variation: Sparkling Nectarine & Blueberry Jellies
Replace the sparkling red wine with $2^1/_4$ cups sparkling peach-flavored wine. Prepare the gelatin and dissolve it in the wine as in the main recipe. Cut the flesh of 2 ripe nectarines into small cubes and sprinkle them with 1 tablespoon lemon juice. Rinse 1 cup blueberries. Put half the blueberries and half the nectarine cubes in the bottom of 6 glasses, then pour over jelly to cover. Let set, then continue as in the main recipe above.

4 sheets of leaf gelatin or 1 package powdered gelatin

2$^1/_4$ cups sparkling Shiraz or other sparkling red wine

2$^2/_3$ cups mixed berries, such as strawberries, raspberries, blackberries, or blueberries

1–2 tablespoons sugar

3–4 tablespoons sugar syrup*

cream or vanilla ice cream, to serve

6 individual glass dishes

Serves 6

Combining chocolate with a strong red wine like Cabernet Sauvignon might sound like an unlikely idea, but if you think about the wine's red berry flavors it makes sense. It also adds an intriguing edge to this dessert that I bet none of your guests will be able to identify. The ideal Cabernet to use is one that is ripe and fruity but not too oaky.

chocolate & cabernet pots

³/₄ **cup fruity Cabernet Sauvignon, preferably from California, Chile, or Australia**

2 tablespoons sugar

7 oz. plain dark chocolate (70 percent cocoa solids)

1¹/₄ **cups light cream**

1 egg

a pinch of ground cinnamon

To serve

2 teaspoons unsweetened cocoa, sifted

confectioners' sugar (optional)

6 or 8 small pots, ramekins, or espresso coffee cups, ¹/₂ *cup each*

Serves 6–8

Put the wine and sugar in a saucepan and heat gently until the sugar has dissolved. Increase the heat very slightly and simmer gently until the wine has reduced by two-thirds to about 3 tablespoons, 20 to 25 minutes.

Meanwhile, break the chocolate into squares, and put them in a blender. Blitz briefly to break them into small pieces.

Put the cream in a saucepan and heat until almost boiling. Pour the hot cream over the chocolate in the blender, then add the hot, sweetened wine. Leave for a few seconds so the chocolate melts. Whizz briefly until the mixture is smooth. Add the egg and cinnamon and whizz again briefly to mix.

Pour the mixture into 6 or 8 ramekins or espresso cups, then chill in the refrigerator for 3 to 4 hours. Remove the chocolate pots from the refrigerator 20 minutes before serving. To serve, sprinkle a thin layer of cocoa powder over the top of each pot, then sprinkle with a little sifted confectioners' sugar, if liked.

Note This dessert contains raw egg, see note on page 4.

Recommended wine match A small glass of vintage character or late-bottled vintage port would work well with these chocolate pots.

Wine can also be used as the basis for delicious drinks—ice-cold ones for summer, warming ones for winter. I like this white sangría even more than the classic red version—it makes a wonderfully refreshing, summery drink.

white sangría

Pour the wine into a large jug or bowl, add the orange-flavored liqueur and sugar, and stir until the sugar has dissolved. Add the orange and lemon slices, cover with plastic wrap, and let infuse in the refrigerator for several hours or overnight.

When ready to serve, add the melon and a couple of handfuls of ice cubes (about 10), then top up with soda water, to taste.

1 bottle inexpensive dry white wine, 750 ml, chilled

$^1/_4$ cup orange-flavored liqueur, such as Cointreau

2 tablespoons sugar

$^1/_2$ orange, thinly sliced

$^1/_2$ lemon, thinly sliced

$^1/_4$ ripe honeydew melon, peeled and cut into cubes

about 10 ice cubes

chilled soda water, to taste

Serves 8–10

If you've never made mulled wine yourself, you should try it. It couldn't be simpler and tastes infinitely better than the ready-mixed versions. The only thing you have to be careful about is that the wine doesn't boil.

my favorite mulled wine

Pour the wine into a large saucepan and add 2 cups cold water. Add the orange, lemon zest, spices, and sugar and heat gently until almost boiling. Reduce the heat as low as possible, the liquid should barely tremble, and simmer for about 30 minutes so the spices infuse thoroughly.

Add the orange liqueur or brandy and reheat gently. Strain into a large, warmed bowl and add the slices of orange. Ladle into small cups or glasses, to serve.

2 bottles medium-bodied fruity red wine, 750 ml each

1 orange, studded with cloves

zest of $^1/_2$ unwaxed lemon

2 cinnamon sticks

6 cardamom pods, lightly crushed

a little freshly grated nutmeg

$^1/_2$ cup brown sugar

$^1/_2$ cup orange-flavored liqueur, such as Cointreau or Grand Marnier, or brandy

a few orange slices, to serve

Serves 14–16

index

conversion charts

Weights and measures have been rounded up or down slightly to make measuring easier.

Volume equivalents:

American	Metric	Imperial
1 teaspoon	5 ml	
1 tablespoon	15 ml	
¼ cup	60 ml	2 fl.oz.
⅓ cup	75 ml	2½ fl.oz.
½ cup	125 ml	4 fl.oz.
⅔ cup	150 ml	5 fl.oz. (¼ pint)
¾ cup	175 ml	6 fl.oz.
1 cup	250 ml	8 fl.oz.

Weight equivalents:

Imperial	Metric
1 oz.	25 g
2 oz.	50 g
3 oz.	75 g
4 oz.	125 g
5 oz.	150 g
6 oz.	175 g
7 oz.	200 g
8 oz. (½ lb.)	250 g
9 oz.	275 g
10 oz.	300 g
11 oz.	325 g
12 oz.	375 g
13 oz.	400 g
14 oz.	425 g
15 oz.	475 g
16 oz. (1 lb.)	500 g
2 lb.	1 kg

Measurements:

Inches	Cm
¼ inch	5 mm
½ inch	1 cm
¾ inch	1.5 cm
1 inch	2.5 cm
2 inches	5 cm
3 inches	7 cm
4 inches	10 cm
5 inches	12 cm
6 inches	15 cm
7 inches	18 cm
8 inches	20 cm
9 inches	23 cm
10 inches	25 cm
11 inches	28 cm
12 inches	30 cm

Oven temperatures:

110°C	(225°F)	Gas ¼
120°C	(250°F)	Gas ½
140°C	(275°F)	Gas 1
150°C	(300°F)	Gas 2
160°C	(325°F)	Gas 3
180°C	(350°F)	Gas 4
190°C	(375°F)	Gas 5
200°C	(400°F)	Gas 6
220°C	(425°F)	Gas 7
230°C	(450°F)	Gas 8
240°C	(475°F)	Gas 9